What are we learning?

What will we learn this week?

New Words

We will learn lots of **words about food**, SOME of the words we will learn are on the next page, but we will learn many more.

Questions (and answers)

We will learn to ask **Do you want a...**We will learn about plurals

More Questions (and answers)

We will learn to ask **Do you like.** We will learn that these questions always use plural forms..

Grammar

We will learn about **different plurals.** How some words have 's' and others have 'es' or nothing.. .

Phonics

We will learn about the the sounds **sh, th and ch** and the **r blends.**

Spelling

We will learn how to spell some of the words we learnt

And Fun!

We will also play lots of games and have lots of fun!

Learn Some Words

Question Time

Do you want a pear?

No, I don't.

Do you want a peach?

Yes, I do.

Can You Do It?

Draw a picture in the box of something you want to eat. Then see if your classmates can guess what you have drawn.

Extension (for high levels)

If it's just one, we say, 'Do you want A ...'

If there is more than one we say, 'Do you want SOME....'

Do you want a cherry?

Do you want some cherries

Trace and Match

Trace, complete and match the questions.

More Words

Did you see? All these words have an 's' at the end. Ask your teacher why!

Let's learn some more words!

Draw the pictures of the words you learned here:

Can you find a:

grapes

pancakes

peaches

hamburgers

and add four more foods you like:

____

____

____

____

____

Now, play a game! Can you jump?

Have Some Fun

Ask your friend a question. Then toss a coin. If it lands 'heads' they must say **'yes, I do'**. If it lands 'tails' they must say **'no, I don't'.** Let's see who has a silly question!

More Questions

Do you like peaches?

No, I don't.

Do you like hamburgers?

Yes, I do

Ask and answer with your friends

Can you do it?

Choose some food and walk around your classroom asking:

Do you like .....?

Who can answer the most questions?

Let's write

Be careful! Is S or ES?

	Do you like chips?	______________
	Do you like ______________?	______________
		______________
		______________
		______________

Have some fun!

On a separate piece of paper write a question and answer. Then cut it up and challenge your friend to put it back together. When you are finished paste your sentence here.

Grammar

Now we should know that when there is more than one we add a 's'.

1 cake

2 cake**s**

But sometimes (ask your teacher when!) we add 'es'

1 peach

2 peach**es**

And sometimes we don't add anything at all!

CANDY!

Practice Time!

You decide. S, ES or NOTHING

apple	________________
peach	________________
candy	________________
box	________________

Have some fun!

Can you run? Your teacher will put lots of pictures on the floor and then will call out a word. You have to run to find the right one – but listen carefully for the 's'!

When you are finished write down all the words you got here:

More fun

Let's play a silly game. Listen to your teacher. He will say a word. If it has an 's' then stand up. If there is no 's' then sit down!

Phonics

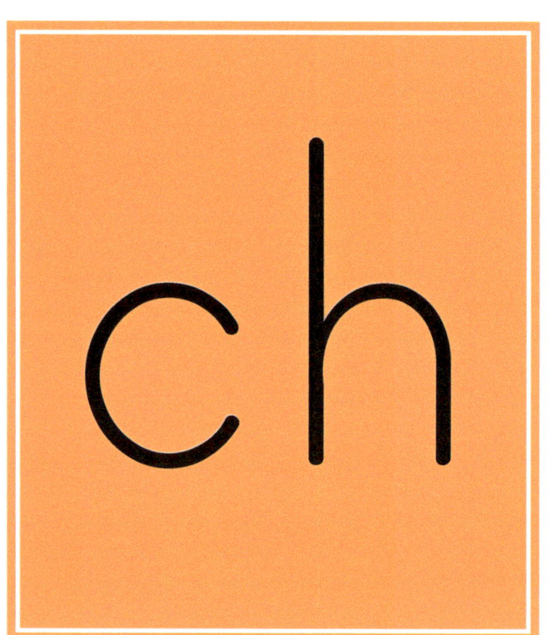

What does this say?

It has two sounds!
Can you read these words?

We see this sound in the word cherry

.

More

And do you remember these sounds?

Play a game

Your teacher will give you lots of 'ch', 'sh' and 'th' words. Try to read them. Then put them into three groups.

How fast can you be?

Practice

Odd one out

Cross out the pictures that do NOT have a 'ch' sound and then write the word under the picture. Then you can color ☺

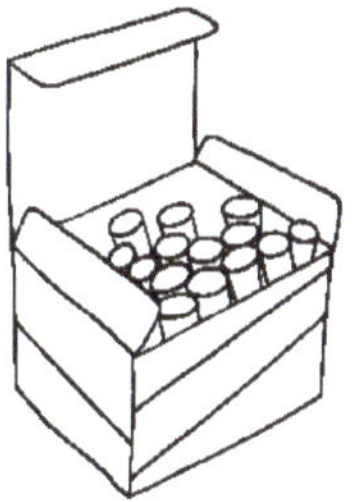

Daily English

Some more yummy food...

Have some fun!

Play Pictionary! Draw a word and see if anyone can guess what you are drawing.

Spelling

Let's practice the words! Please LOOK, COVER, WRITE and CHECK every day!

	Monday	Tuesday	Wednesday	Thursday
a chip				
a cherry				
a peach				
a cake				
a lollypop				
a lemon				
candy				
crackers				

a

Phonics (2)

What does this say?

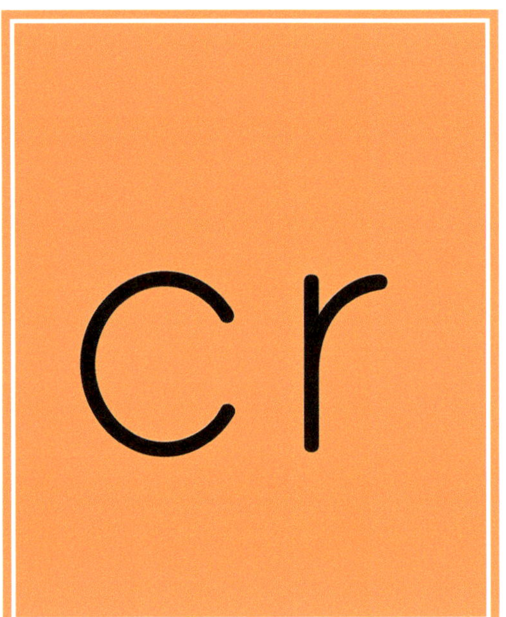

We see this sound in

crackers

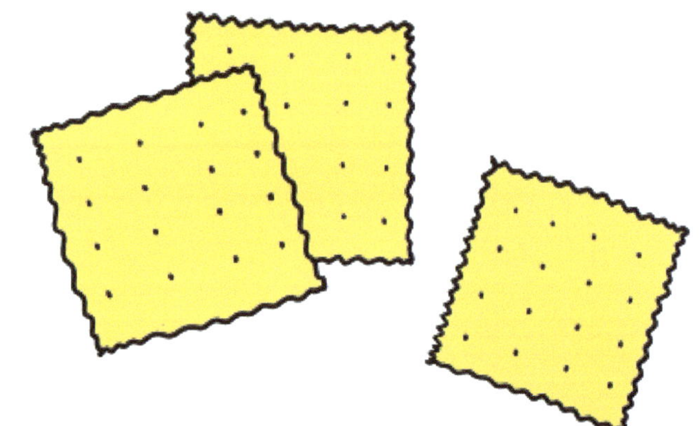

Learn More

Take a letter C and a letter R read it.

Then change the C to a F what does it say now?

Then change the C to a B what does it say now?

Practice

Change a letter

Can you read this word?

p r a y

Now, cut out the letters below and put them over the 'p' – what new words have you made, can you read them all? Which ones are real words?

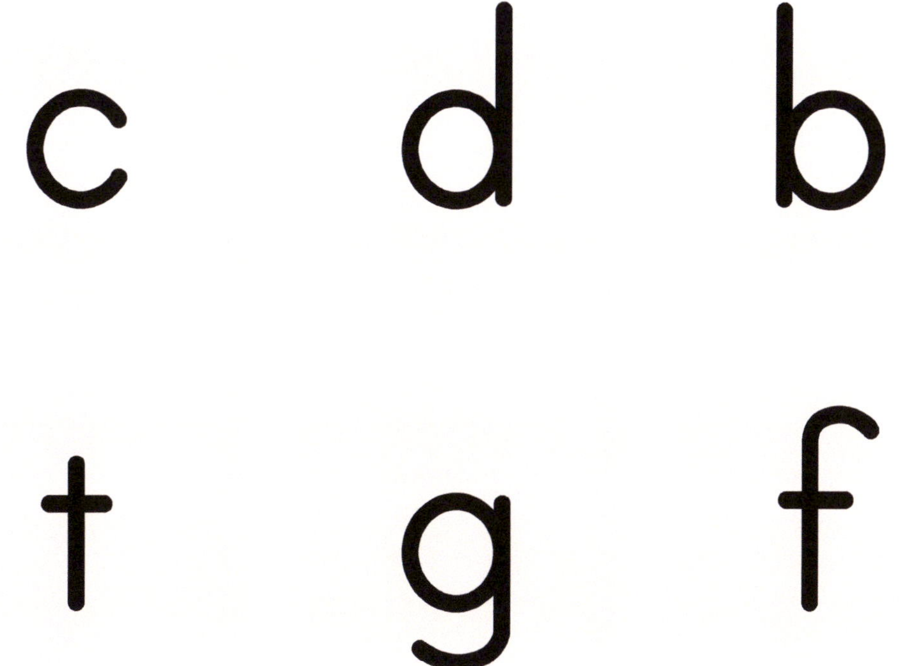

Practice

Change a letter

Now write all the words you made here:

Can you make a sentence with each word?

Homework (1)

Homework (2)

How many words can you find? Write them below.

S	R	A	C	H	I	P	W	U	W	A	S	N	H	N
Z	I	U	T	K	R	S	Z	B	S	E	P	A	R	G
T	A	N	C	D	N	A	S	F	K	C	B	T	S	H
I	M	W	P	O	J	G	E	A	S	W	Z	K	G	Y
S	K	K	M	G	P	D	C	P	E	C	Y	I	C	B
T	R	E	L	M	M	N	C	O	H	R	O	I	I	H
K	L	E	E	J	A	V	T	P	C	A	Y	R	G	N
A	E	D	G	P	T	Q	K	Y	A	C	Y	A	N	M
K	M	Z	W	R	W	J	A	L	E	K	U	W	B	M
C	V	A	V	C	U	M	P	L	P	E	T	M	W	H
E	U	T	P	M	S	B	V	O	Q	R	D	U	U	T
L	K	X	B	E	I	T	M	L	H	S	M	L	F	A
I	L	A	L	C	A	T	N	A	B	O	Z	F	J	N
Y	Q	R	C	D	B	C	E	D	H	S	R	O	C	W
Z	R	U	V	A	U	N	H	A	C	H	E	R	R	Y

Have some fun!

You've worked hard, now it is time to have some fun! We are going to COOK!

What did you cook?

I cooked a _________________________

How did you cook it?

____

____

More writing

If you need any more space to write, then use these pages

Mini Flashcards

a peach	a chip
crackers	a cake
candy	a cherry
a lemon	a lollypop

Don't lose them!

Put your mini flashcards here once you have cut them out

Completion of
Mark's Mad Holiday
This certificate is presented to
For completing the 'Food' unit
BUS 10
SCHOOL
Crayons
ABC
DE

http://ezbooks.me

ezBooks

Regal Court Business Centre

Tian He

Guangzhou

China

Mark's Mad Holidays Level 3 - Food Unit

First published March 2013

ISBN 978-1-300-68157-1

Project Manager: Mark Revis

Art Editor: Betty Long

Production Manager: Tara Chen

www.ingramcontent.com/pod-product-compliance
Ingram Content Group UK Ltd.
Pitfield, Milton Keynes, MK11 3LW, UK
UKHW060122300726
14090UKWH00002B/314

* 9 7 8 1 3 0 0 6 8 1 5 7 1 *